SOUTHAMPTON

THROUGH THIS CENTURY

By
Eric Wyeth Gadd

Published by PAUL CAVE PUBLICATIONS LTD.,
74 Bedford Place, Southampton.

Printed by Brown and Son (Ringwood) Ltd.

By the same Author:

Paul Cave Publications Ltd.

Southampton — 100 Years Ago
Southampton in the 'Twenties
The Changing Face of Southampton
Hampshire Evacuees

K.A.F. Brewin Books.

Victorian Logs

Cover picture:
Above Bar in the 1930's.

©

E. W. G.
and
P. C.

ISBN 0-86146-068-5

Published: October 1988

CONTENTS   PAGE

AUTHOR'S PREFACE

Ever since I began to write about life in the past I have been discovering how many readers share my interests. From friends — many of them complete strangers — an ever-growing collection of letters has been adding to one's store of knowledge, suggesting answers to queries, gently pointing out one's errors and, in general, offering encouragement for further research and writing.

Surprisingly, these contacts have come, not only from Southampton and its immediate neighbourhood, but from many other parts of the British Isles, and even from overseas.

This is all most gratifying, but there is more to tell. Many well-wishers have added to my collection of photographs and other material by loans and, in many cases, outright gifts. Without such generosity this book would never have been written. It is with the greatest pleasure that I take this opportunity of thanking all these kind friends for their contributions. (One name I cannot repeat: that of the good soul who supplied one of the finest photographs in the book, who insisted, for personal reasons, upon remaining anonymous).

Grateful thanks then to: Mesdames D. M. Frost, A. Goodchild, M. Green, S. Hodges, E. G. Price, J. Sandford, A. Stacey, E. Travis, A. Williams, the late Mrs. E. Whitehorn; Misses H. Warner and J. B. Wood; A. W. Cooper, G. Day, J. G. Espezel, the Rev. G. Fuller, the late Mr. N. Gardiner, R. P. Hoare, A. R. House, J. Kimber, C. Lanham, the late Mr. P. Lilley, B. R. Mackay, D. J. Martin, T. A. May, A. R. Paine, R. C. Payne, G. Playdon, M. L. Rood, the late Mr. C. Saunders, C. J. Shepperd, R. F. Shepperd, R. W. Stickland, J. Stockley, M. Tighe, A. J. Warren, H. L. Wyeth; the Headmaster, Foundry Lane School, Associated British Ports, Bitterne Local History Society, Hill College, J. Mowlem & Co., Plc, Edmund Nuttall Ltd., Southampton City Records Office, Southampton City Museums, Southampton City Reference Library, Southampton University Library, Southampton University Industrial Archaeological Group, the Southern Evening Echo.

My appreciation must be expressed, too, for the photographic expertise of Mr. Bob Thomas and Mr. Gerry Walden.

If I have omitted any names which should have been included, I tender my sincere apologies.

E.W.G.

THE BACKWARD GLANCE
FAMILY FOCUS

The past 50 years have seen a quiet revolution. Thousands of families have moved out of the kitchen. Formerly, for many, life had been lived in the back of the house. The 'front room' or parlour, largely neglected, was a humble sort of museum, dominated by anti-macassars and aspidistras, a marble clock and the large gilt-framed pictures, with Goss china and late Victorian ornaments on the mantlepiece and the whatnot in the corner.

The shiny brass fire-irons were never used. On special occasions a fire in the little grate was fed from a dingy scuttle with a drab iron shovel and poked with a workmanlike kitchen poker.

Apart from the odd Sunday or the occasional visit from relatives, the front room came into its own only at Christmas time. Then the paper-chains, home made from ha'penny packets bought from the local newsagent, were hung from corner to corner (carefully keeping clear of the gas-bracket). Christmas cards stood among the knick-knacks on the mantlepiece; sprigs of holly peeped out from behind the edges of the over-mantel and there might even be a scrap of mistletoe dangling saucily over the doorway. Christmas trees, nowadays universal, were rarely seen.

For many, Christmas dinner (back in the kitchen) was likely to feature roast beef, pork or chicken, though duck or goose were favoured by some. Christmas pudding and mince pies were obligatory. Tea time: jelly and blancmange and Christmas cake, but at least a token intake of bread and butter was insisted upon.

Normally then the family lived in the warm, cosy little room at the back of the house. Its centre and focus was the kitchen table, whose plain deal top, frequently scrubbed, was usually hidden beneath a green baize cover fringed with tassels.

Here we youngsters played our games — ludo, snakes and ladders, draughts, dominoes, the simpler card games — but never on Sundays. Here homework was wrestled with. Here Mother carefully cut around the edges of flimsy brown paper patterns pinned to dress material brought home from Edwin Jones' or McIlroy's in East Street.

Here one sorted out foreign stamps — 'swaps' excitedly brought home from school. Here one pored over books from the school library — Ballantyne or Henty, Jules Verne or H. G. Wells, Jerome K. Jerome or W. W. Jacobs, Conan

Doyle or Baroness Orczy.

To me, however, the greatest joy was Arthur Mee's 'Children's Encyclopaedia'. A kind relative had given me the complete work. Endless delight.

On the kitchen table we constructed our 'peep-shows'. Mounted in a boot-box was arranged a number of cut-out figures and objects. The lid was replaced by a sheet of coloured tissue paper and a peep-hole was made at one end. To this day I cannot bear to throw away an empty shoe-box.

More ambitious was a toy theatre, complete with curtains, actors, painted scenery. Another favourite was a helter-skelter, made from an empty cereal packet, with elaborate runways linking the entrance at the top with the exit at

Edwin Jones' Great East Street store.

The tram took Mum to town and back.

the base; given careful construction, a marble made the journey without mishap.

That wonderful invention, Meccano, since superseded by even cleverer ideas, kept lively boys quiet for hours. When a girl tired of playing with her toy post-office or her toy sweet-shop she turned joyfully to her beloved family of dolls.

How proud I was when I was able to invite my friends in to see my magic lantern. The gas was turned down and the pictures were projected on to a sheet pinned to the wall. What if the thing smoked and smelled? Who cared?

Today's sophisticated youngsters will smile indulgently at the naivety of it all. How could one know how different life would be half a century later?

DOCKSIDE TRIUMPH

A short while ago, turning out a cupboard which had long been left undisturbed, I came across a copy, published during the early 1930s, of the excellent magazine 'The Studio'. In it was a four-page article, illustrated by beautifully-produced pencil drawings by Sydney R. Jones, entitled 'The New Southern Railway Graving Dock at Southampton'.

To most of Southampton's people the story of the city's docks is a closed book, yet no other single factor has contributed as much to the welfare of the local community during the past century and a half.

Looking landwards from the entrance, June, 1932.

The Great West Wall, October, 1932.

From the acquisition in 1836 of 216 acres of land, mostly tidal mudflats lying off the peninsula between the Test and the Itchen, and the construction during the following six years of the outer docks, development has proceeded — sometimes slowly, sometimes at breathtaking pace.

No period has seen such a remarkable transformation as the seven years from 1927, during which the new Western Docks complex was built. This entailed the reclamation between the Royal Pier and Millbrook Point of 400 acres of tidal foreshore (an area larger than Southampton Common) and the dumping of millions of tons of mud behind a massive seawall, to allow for the provision of 1½ miles of quays.

The crowning achievement was the subject of my rediscovered article, the construction of the gigantic graving dock, named after King George V and opened by him in 1934.

The many far-reaching changes of more recent years can do nothing to detract from this triumph of half a century ago.

With the kind permission of the contractors (Edmund Nuttall Ltd and J. Mowlem & Co. PLC) the original drawings are reproduced here and, in the interests of the technically-minded, the accompanying description is added:

"It was an excellent idea of the contractors to record the progress of the construction of the recently opened graving dock, built at Southampton for the Southern Railway, through drawings by Sydney R. Jones. No trace now remains of the constructional work and, therefore, the drawings have an added value.

This new Southern Railway dock is the largest thing of its kind in the world. It is 400 yards in length and 50½ feet in depth. The dock has a sliding caisson at the entrance which permits it to be used either wet or dry. It is constructed mainly of concrete, and is a magnificent example of modern big-scale engineering and building enterprise.

The successful accomplishment of the construction of this dock necessitated the development of plant which had to be designed specially. The giant mixers needed to supply concrete in sufficient quantity were indeed fed, not with sacks, but with train loads of cement, and the work progressed continuously night and day for two years.

During this time a continuous series of varied and impressive effects was presented, though, of course, each was of only transitory character. The ever-changing forms and masses, the moving machinery, rapid excavation and the manipulation of the concrete and of the special mixing plant, have unfolded aspects filled not only with pictorial significance but with the very spirit of modern engineering."

Auxiliary concrete mixer at the Dock entrance.

A GARDEN SUBURB IS BORN

The story of the Chessel estate at Bitterne has been told a number of times. Yet by relating the present with the past, by making good use of retentive memories and by consulting old maps, we may follow trails little explored before.

First, a brief reminder of the estate's history. In the 18th century — Southampton's 'Spa Period' — many well-to-do families, drawn by the attractions of the countryside surrounding the town, chose the high ground to the east of the Itchen for the building of gracious mansions set in generous park lands. Thus in 1797 David Lance built Chessel House on a large piece of land bounded by Northam Bridge Road (now Bitterne Road), that part of the road now named Pear Tree Avenue as far as the south-west tip of Freemantle Common, and the foreshore of the river. Much of the estate was enclosed within high brick walls.

In 1808, Jane Austen, then living in Southampton, took the ferry to Itchen and walked by way of Pear Tree Green to pay a courtesy call on the Lances. Still on foot, she returned to her home in Castle Square, crossing the first Northam

Chessel House and drive viewed from the west.

·The Bitterne Road lodge

Bridge, which had been opened only a few years earlier.

In 1820 the estate passed to Lord Ashtown and 20 years later to Sir William Richardson and his heirs. In 1910 it was sold for commercial development.

What of Chessel House itself? Within living memory the impressive building stood on the direct link between the modern Chessel Avenue/Pear Tree Avenue junction and the bottom of modern Athelstan Road. The lower end of this drive (long since vanished) was by way of an embankment, pierced by a tunnel to allow cattle to move freely between the meadows on either side.

The upper entrance to the gravelled drive was through iron gates set between stone pillars. These still stand, today more widely separated, to cope with modern traffic. The lodge cottage just here has survived; it is now named Magellan.

In the eighteenth century an expert in the planning of noble estates wrote: "The drive to the house should curve gracefully." Sure enough, from an old map we find, to our surprise, that from these stone pillars the visitors' carriages once followed a gentle anti-clockwise arc before pulling up at Chessel House's main entrance. Soon this was changed to a direct tree-lined drive — the line of modern Chessel Avenue.

The other two lodges — one near the high exit to modern Athelstan Road, the other opposite the lower end of the Midanbury Lane — have disappeared.

The estate farm stood a few hundred yards down the main drive. This remained in active life for several years after the area was opened up to the public, and many families on their favourite Sunday stroll would pause there, but taking care not to approach too near, for the place was guarded by dogs — and geese! The children were disappointed if the strutting peacocks failed to appear.

Today one is tempted to wonder whether a number of excellent old fruit trees, still vigorous, in back gardens known to be on the site of the farm, are surviving links with those distant days.

Behind the farm ran a gravel path which led to the Northam Bridge Road thatched lodge. This path was edged by black iron fencing, beyond which a large meadow sloped steeply away — land later to become Chessel Crescent.

Some years ago the owner of No. 64 Chessel Avenue was puzzled to find a streak of gravel running diagonally, just beneath the surface, in his lawn. A neighbour with a good memory was able to point out that this was a relic of the old pathway, for certain.

Estate developers often have changes of mind after work on development has begun. We find that Fox and Sons' original plans differ in many details from the final layout of the estate. Lower Chessel Avenue was first planned as a widening of the gravel footpath, mentioned above, but in view of the contours this idea would have been impractable and was abandoned. then Athelstan Road had not been scheduled to extend beyond its junction with Bitterne Way, for its progress had been blocked by the dense, attractive Redmoor Copse. However, this was removed long ago to make way for housing and one of the steepest stretches of road in the whole of Southampton.

We are all familiar with the extravagant jargon used by some estate agents, but in 1910 there was no need to exceed the plain truth in claims on behalf of "Chessel House Estate — Southampton's Garden Suburb". Here were delightful slopes; wooded hills; invigorating country air; above all, magnificent views, many of which over the years have proved indestructible.

Opposite: The plan for the Chessel House Estate

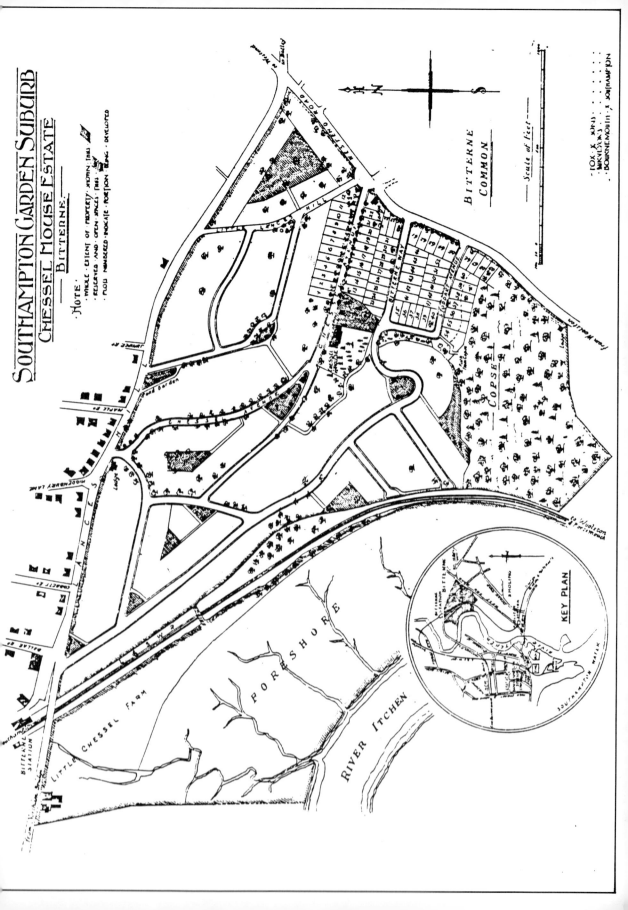

SOUTHAMPTON'S GROWING PAINS

Strikes, lock-outs, protests, demonstrations. These terms send one's thoughts to the great industrial centres of the country. Yet in Southampton's story during the past hundred years we find industrial disturbances, many bitter, some even violent.

Not surprisingly, many of such conflicts centred on dockland. In 1872 was the first serious attempt to combat the pitiable wages of seamen. When the men struck for better conditions there were several ugly confrontations with authority — even alarming rumours of plans for armed attempts to set fire to shipping and, if thwarted, to spill human blood! However, the action, hasty and ill-organised, fizzled out in failure, leaving a legacy of fierce recrimination.

Two years later a strike by shipwrights for an increase in pay ended in no greater satisfaction.

During a quiet period of more than a decade, working men everywhere were coming to realise their potential power, and a successful strike by London dockers encouraged the Southampton men to demand better wages, despite their employers' shaky financial position. Defying an unhelpful response, the men struck, pickets were posted in Canute Road and traffic into the docks, including trains, was halted. When roughs joined the strikers the police were overwhelmed, and the Mayor read the Riot Act. Troops sent from Portsmouth tried to clear the road, but were greeted with hails of stones. Bayonets were fixed and ammunition issued, but the Mayor kept his head. He ordered the Fire Brigade to attack with hoses, and the street was quickly cleared.

A sequel: that night the Mayor's boot-shop in East Street was partially demolished.

Next day troops had to deal with further outbursts of violence; two gunboats and a torpedo-boat arrived from Portsmouth to prevent pickets invading the docks by water and a warning was issued that the soldiers would fire if necessary.

Humiliation followed. The national union refused to back this unofficial strike and the men had to return to work with little achieved. Several rioters (including one local strike-leader) were sent to jail.

The century closed in the town without more unseemly incidents, though working conditions and wages in many trades were, by later standards, deplorable.

The winter of 1903-4 was probably the most distressing of all, with hundreds

Bakers' strike — queue at a Bitterne Park family bakery — 5th August, 1919

of men out of work.

The years 1911 and 1912 were unique in having strikes from seamen and firemen, stevedores, shipwrights, plumbers, coal-porters, general labourers, painters, engineers, carpenters and joiners.

At worst the general public were affected only indirectly by these struggles, but several years later there were conflicts, each of which had an impact upon the smooth routine of many homes.

In 1919 Corporation labourers struck without warning, having been denied an addition of five shillings to their £1 war bonus. The result was interference with the town's water supply, with refuse collection, the sweeping of the streets, the disposal of sewage and the digging of graves. After three days of worrying crisis, the men's demands were met.

Within a week the bakers struck for more pay. There were then a number of family bakeries, whose owners — to the dismay of the strikers — worked like Trojans to ease the situation; shops took in extra supplies of flour and yeast, and many housewives turned to home baking. Even so, before settlement, many townspeople suffered four days of inconvenience.

In 1920 the dismissal of a tram conductor precipitated a tram strike, and Southampton took to the streets. For nine days, after breakfast and at tea-time, pavements became crowded and the town's cycle-mindedness became more evident than ever.

Two years later there was Southampton's famous 1922 teachers' strike (lock-out?), which closed the schools for 14 weeks.

20th July, 1919 — Trade Union demonstration on the Common

Local unrest was not confined to strikes. Political opinion in the country
was deeply divided by the Russian revolution of 1917-18. The Establishment's
sympathies were with the old order, and troops and supplies were sent to
help combat 'the Red Menace'. In 1919 the Left, feeling an uneasy kinship
with the rebels, mounted a nationwide campaign of protest against the action

of the government. Southampton's faithful assembled on 20th July in Queens Park and marched with bands and banners to the Common. Socialist speaker Ben Tillett was backed by three ardent locals — 'Tommy' Lewis, Emily Palmer and Ralph Morley.

We are rightly concerned today about widespread unemployment, but there were 3¾ million out of work in 1932, when the population had reached only four-fifths of the present level. Then, to the loss of morale of the unemployed, was added a degree of poverty unknown nowadays. Our picture

shows a section of the 1,400 Southampton workless men who gathered on 19th October, 1932 outside the Audit House (then the seat of local government) in protest at their lot.

THE TRIANGLE SCORES A CENTURY

Immediately after the opening in 1883 of Southampton's first Cobden Bridge the development of the Bitterne Park estate began. This was a challenging project, for the land, partly farmland, partly woods and partly scrub, rose steeply to the imposing heights of Middenbury, to use its old spelling.

Developers' plans for the layout of new estates are often modified in the cold light of practice, but we find that the original street plan, which still exists, differs little from the final result which we know today.

One section of this map has been followed exactly. From the point where the new bridge joined the eastern river bank, Manor Farm Road runs north, Whitworth Crescent (then named Whitworth Road) runs south and Cobden Avenue, veering slightly, continues the line of the bridge. At the junction so formed the old map shows a triangle, within which we find a neat square, boldly marked 'Estate Office'. Here would have been found Alfred Chafen, Senior, agent for the Liberal Land Company (donors of the new bridge).

This gentleman was soon closely identified with the social and religious life of the growing district. His name is perpetuated in Chafen Road, Bitterne Manor.

That tiny triangle was destined to become the focal point of life in the fast-developing suburb.

First, the road adjacent to the Triangle immediately became the recognised shopping centre, with bank, post office, Co-op, butchers, bakers, grocers, confectioners, a newsagent, a chemist, a fishmonger, a dairy, a draper, an outfitter, an ironmonger, a cobbler, a jeweller, a coal merchant, a fruiterer — and a new pub nearby. Other shops soon followed.

Then the spot was a tram terminus. Here mothers began their trips to town (via High Street or St. Mary's — twopence either way). Here the few non-cycling fathers set out for work, many using the special workman's ticket. Here, too, a tram conductor would pull on a rope and swing his trolley-pole into reverse, ready for the return journey, while small boys watched fascinated, secretly hoping that the chap would be clumsy and create a multitude of sparks from the overhead wire (the tram lines were not extended to the bottom of Bullar Road until 1923).

The Triangle was a social centre. Within its low iron railings bands would play to appreciative crowds on summer evenings, and as election days approached, aspirants to municipal or parliamentary honours would mount soap-boxes. On Empire Day, 1910 Headmaster 'Dad' Cleary and his boys ended their march round the district, led by their very own fife and drum band, with patriotic songs at the Triangle.

The conductor has not yet swung his trolley pole for the return journey.

Shops at Bitterne Park Triangle, early in this century

Almost exactly 50 years had passed since that little three-cornered piece of ground had been left, insignificant, untidy, at the meeting-place of the new bridge and the three rough, gravelly roads. In that half-century the little patch

The Bitterne Park Triangle

had been tidied, turfed, planted and fenced. The insignificant had taken on significance, had become an integral feature in the life of a lively community. The triangle had become the Triangle. Indeed, that name was by now applied by tacit agreement to the whole of the busy shopping centre.

Just when the half-century had been reached, Authority took a decision. Corporation workmen removed the fence, dug up the shrubs, sliced up the turf. Men with tapes measured with scrupulous care. Pegs were driven, deep trenches dug. Concrete was poured in, carefully numbered stones were unloaded from lorries and set in position, checked and re-checked. Southampton's famous landmark, the Clock Tower, which had stood since Victorian times at the junction of Above Bar and New Road, was re-erected at Bitterne Park's Triangle.

That was in 1935, so now another half-century has passed. The old monument still stands — slightly tilting. It is more than a useful time-piece. It is a reminder of a more leisurely age when, on a hot summer's day, weary horses could pause for respite and — innocent of thoughts of hygiene — grubby urchins could slake their thirsts from chained iron mugs. Trough and basin have long since been cemented over.

The worthy citizens of Bitterne Park have a small grievance. After 100 years they regard The Triangle as part of their special heritage. Yet they frequently hear and read references to the Bitterne Triangle. But from here, at the heart of Bitterne Park, the heart of Bitterne is a mile away. Bitterne has its own cherished traditions. Let Bitterne Park keep its century-old heritage unimpaired.

PRECIOUS RESPITE

When every weekday was a workday and every workday was long, a family holiday at the seaside was an experience to be relished to the full.

First there was the excited tramp along the resounding planks of Southampton's Royal Pier; the descent of the covered way that led down to the little paddle-steamer; the pontoon whose gentle pitching gave a brief foretaste of the joys ahead; aboard, the choice of a good place to sit (a place which would never be occupied for long); the spotless, scrubbed decks and the gleaming brasswork.

Slowly we turn about. Impudently our tiny craft passes her great ocean sisters as they prepare for their voyages to Cape Town or Melbourne, New York or Rio or Bombay. Towering cranes unload bulky crates; huge nets filled with cabin trunks swoop aloft before descending unerringly into cavernous holds.

We pass Hythe Pier; Netley Hospital, its dome glinting in the sunshine. High above us, friendly crewmen, leaning on the rails of liners just arriving or just departing, look down and wave. Flattered, we respond.

We go down to the engine room where, enthralled, we watch the humming, throbbing wheels, great and small, and the quaint little gadgets which furtively bob up and down in odd corners; we savour the warm, oily smell of the place.

As we approach Calshot Castle, we lessen speed and the threshing of those wheels ceases for a few moments, for shore contact has to be made by a small boat. Packages and cheery greetings are exchanged.

Every minute brings something of interest. A grimy dredger slogs away at its dull but vital task. A gaunt cormorant is perched sure-clawed on the top of a dancing buoy. Passengers rush excitedly to the side, where three porpoises are cavorting merrily.

On the top deck there is sudden laughter. A young man, with red face and sheepish grin, gazes ruefully astern, where his straw boater dances happily up and down in the sea.

And never deserting us, the seagulls scream and swoop.

Cowes at last! We struggle up (or down) the narrow gangway with our luggage.

For an extended stay, Sandown is our favourite. We don't spend all our time on the beach: to our family, walking is second nature, so the cliff path to Shanklin is routine. When Culver Cliff beckons, we discover that the distance is deceptive, but we press on.

In the evenings we listen to the smart gold-braided band, or stroll along the

The "Duchess of Fife" prepares to leave for the island.

prom, slackening our pace as we reach the open lawns of the Ocean Hotel ("We mustn't stop — It's rude to stare!"). Here the well-to-do in full evening dress sit at little tables with their glasses of wine and their cigars, and sometimes a lady may be seen with a cigarette!

I had never heard then of Disraeli's 'Two Worlds', but I know now what he meant. That world of hotels was one which I was quite sure I would never enter.

Once or twice during the holiday we go to see the concert party on the pier. Many entertainers, later to become household names, served their apprenticeships with those seaside concert parties.

Dotted at intervals along the prom there were barrow-boys, with funny hats, or 'blowers' which uncoiled as one blows, or lucky bags, or faintly rude postcards of fat lady bathers with enormous bottoms. The swarthy

COWES (Isle of Wight). — The Royal Yacht Squadron Clubhouse. — Looking East. —

The Royal Yacht Squadron Clubhouse: Regatta Time

moustachioed man with the garishly painted ice-cream barrow ('Cornets a penny, wafers twopence!') was always busy.

Meanwhile on the beach Mums and Dads relaxed in their deckchairs. A dad might undo the waistcoat buttons of his sober best suit — even remove his stiff double collar and tie. If he took off his hat it would probably be replaced by a handkerchief knotted at the corners, for at all costs one must guard against the dreaded sunstroke.

Paddlers outnumbered bathers. Nobody dreamt of undressing on the beach (It was officially forbidden, anyway) and only the genuine enthusiast would face the dreary, smelly bathing machine.

A holiday in the Isle of Wight did not necessarily mean the seaside. We were fortunate in having among our friends a family who lived in a farm cottage just off the Cowes-Newport road, so we were able to enjoy the best of two worlds — seaside and country.

We could lean over the side of the pigsty and carry on a snorty conversation with its tenants; watch the cows being milked; gather the eggs, still warm, from the nest boxes; fetch ice-cold water from the pump; persuade ourselves that our presence in the hay-field was of some help; bravely pat the majestic horses; picnic on the grassy hillside that sloped down to the Medina; wander along narrow winding lanes between high hedges spangled with honeysuckle and dogrose.

The ideal time to stay in or near Cowes was, of course, during The Week.

After so many years, one can still recapture the thrill of rubbing shoulders in that quaint, winding High Street with people from another sphere — the titled, the rich, the famous. Even so, despite the proximity, one was painfully conscious of the unbridgeable gulf which separated these people from us ordinary folk.

1   SANDOWN (Isle of Wight).
The Bay and Pier. — LL.

Sandown's beach with its bathing machines and Culver Cliff in the distance.

28

Aboard the "Britannia," King George V, the Duchess of York (later Elizabeth the Queen Mother) and Earl Jellicoe at Cowes.

Down to the water. Here we had a piece of good fortune far beyond our wildest dreams. We had suddenly become aware of a subdued hum of excitement. Without really knowing why, we had joined the hurrying throng and found ourselves caught up behind the barrier erected to keep the likes of us from the entrance to the sacred Royal Yacht Squadron. Then scarcely believing, we understood. His Majesty King George V was coming ashore. He passed us, almost within touching distance, and he looked neither to the left nor the right.

What an ordinary-looking little man, we thought.

All were utterly silent. No cheering, no tiny Union Jacks, no toddlers tightly gripping posies of flowers, no smiles, no handshakes, no walk-abouts. Several generations would pass before such demonstrations would become commonplace — before solemn awe would give way to uninhibited affection.

What holiday can compare with one which ends, as it began, with a mini-sea-trip? We see again the old familiar sights along the verges of Southampton Water; having passed too close to an outgoing tramp-ship, we pitch and toss to the anxious squeals of old ladies mingled with the youngsters' cries of delight; the sea-gulls again swoop and scream; we gaze in wonder at the waiting ocean giants (the Olympic maybe, or the Aquitania or the Mauretania or the lavender-hued beauty of the Union Castle boats); we tread the gangway; gain the swaying pontoon; tramp along the resounding boards of the Royal Pier.

To young ears even the rattling tram seems to echo the greeting 'Welcome home!'

The Royal Pier — home again!

BY BIKE OR BY TRAM

In the days when people stopped in their tracks to gaze at the sight of a motor-car chugging along the street, the scene was dominated by the horse, the bicycle and, in the town, the tramcar.

Southampton was very much a cycling town. Almost everyone had a bike.

The bobby, in peaked cap and greatcoat, rode his high-framed Sunbeam. The dignified professional man pedalled along the Avenue between home and down-town shop or office. The doctor sped on two wheels between patients. The parson leaned his machine against his elderly parishioner's front garden wall. The awesome headmaster and his cap-touching pupil, "with satchel and shining morning face", dismounted together at the school gate as the summoning bell approached 9 o'clock. The suburban lady sat demurely behind her capacious wicker basket, her skirts protected by smart black chain-case and strings radiating from the rear hub. The lively young blade, crouching low over drop handle-bars, wove expertly in and out between horse-drawn vehicles and tramcars. The labourer, setting out for work (before daylight in the winter), paused to tie his bread and cheese lunch to the carrier at the back of his ancient mount.

Some common sights from those days; enthusiasts bowling along country lanes in groups on visits to beauty spots. An unfortunate fellow kneels beside his upturned bike; an inner tube is immersed in a bowl of water, begged from a nearby wayside cottage. Gravelly roads ensured that a saddle-bag was seldom without a puncture-repairing outfit in its flat metal box. A middle-aged man, his hand on the rear of the saddle (temporarily lowered) pants along behind a wobbly learner, perhaps his wife or child. Nowadays people are not taught to ride; they just teach themselves on fairy-cycles.

A cyclist mounts his machine by the step. As he leans forward, grasping the handle-bars, he places his left foot on this little metal bar attached to the rear hub; he scuffs the ground with his right foot and, as the bike moves forward, he hoists himself aloft and descends, without much dignity, into the saddle. This solemn ritual is clearly a relic from fixed-wheel — or even penny-farthing — days.

In the town's main streets bikes by the dozen stand at the kerb-edges, propped up on one pedal, while their owners complete their shopping at leisure. Few machines are secured by safety-chain or padlock. Detachable pumps, lamps (oil, acetylene or battery), bells, saddle-bags, packages in baskets or on carriers are confidently left and seldom touched (from the distance of our modern lawless days, a sobering thought).

And a sound never heard today — the tinkle of the bicycle bell.

Among prominent Southampton citizens who, before the motor-car came to order their lives, regularly rode cycles, we find Lewis Parkhouse the jeweller, Ronald Shepherd of Shepherd & Hedger, the Rev. H. T. Spencer of Avenue Congregational Church, George Parker (councillor, guardian, 'character') and solicitor John Stephens (Stephens Locke and Abel).

Among the cycling doctors were burly, genial Dr. Stancomb, Dr. Havers of Portswood and Dr. Knowlton of Bitterne. The head of a highly-respected medical family, Dr. Alexander MacKeith, set out every morning from his home in Howard Road in his carriage and then completed his calls in the afternoon by push-bike. Young Dr. Frank Ives made his rounds by cycle, while his father, the dapper 'Dr. Billy', of Portswood Park, travelled grandly behind his top-hatted coachman.

Most people who were not cyclists used the trams. Owing to the difficulties created by having to negotiate the central archway of the Bargate, most trams were open-topped so that when the weather was bad the interiors could become unbearably crowded.

On the upper deck the seats were usually adjustable to the direction of travel. Downstairs one sat facing one's fellow-travellers and this could be an embarrassing experience. There is a story of a fascinated small boy who was asked by the enormously fat man sitting opposite, "Why do you keep staring at me?" The poor lad could only stammer, "C-cos there's nowhere else to look."

Among tram travellers we find notable citizens of the day: S. G. Kimber; "Tommy" Lewis; R. R. Linthorne, the Town Clerk; Mr. Emanuel, the Coroner; Henry Lashmore, of the "Southampton Times"; unique William Burrough Hill; J. W. Sandell, the shipping agent; hearty P. V. Bowyer (Mayor in 1926), who deserted the family tradition of pilotage to become an estate agent.

Back to bikes: one life-long cyclist was Seymour J. Gubb, a great headmaster of Taunton's School. On retiring in 1924 he was presented with a Morris Cowley motor-car.

Bargate, bikes and boaters (straw hats)

Saturday afternoons in the 1920's — off to the country

SUNDAY-BEST DAYS

One of life's pleasures for our ancestors — and we need go back no further than two generations — was the frequently recurring opportunity of simply coming together. Few experiences gave greater satisfaction to Mr. and Mrs. Southampton than donning their Sunday best for a Special Occasion. For those with homes in the suburbs, this would usually mean a twopenny tram-ride; for the hundreds who lived centrally, a stroll down the street or across the parks. Occasionally there might be an exciting trip to the outskirts of the town.

It could be the opening of a new building; or the civic reception of a V.I.P.; or a sight of troops encamped on the Common; or a regatta off the Royal Pier; or an historical pageant in which proud citizens, arrayed in colourful costumes, processed through the High Street, Above Bar and St. Mary Street; or a welcome to May Day; or the conferment of the Freedom of the Borough upon a distinguished figure; or even a reverent memorial service.

Stone-laying ceremonies were especial favourites. Our first picture was taken on 6th March, 1900, when the foundation stone of the new Workhouse Infirmary was laid at Shirley Warren. This was the initial step in the long journey to the establishment of today's gigantic General Hospital.

Two fashion notes: many silk hats had been taken out of their boxes and brushed that day — and then we notice the striking contrast between the grim 'uniforms' of the children on the left (obviously from a local orphanage or some such institution) and the sumptuous garments of the young ladies on the right.

Our next picture was taken the following year, when a prominent member of the local School Board, Mr. John Hunt, laid the foundation stone of Foundry Lane School, (the worthy gentleman is seen wearing a grey topper and holding a silver trowel).

It is known that the Hampshire Volunteer Infantry Brigade bivouacked on the Common in September, 1903. As our third photograph appeared on a post-card posted in 1904, it seems likely that it was taken during a church parade at that time. The foreground is dominated by straw hats, the distance by bell-tents.

The period following World War I was an especially busy time for the photographers, despite the burden of cumbersome cameras.

In April, 1919 the townspeople invaded Above Bar en masse to honour their own V.C., Lieutenant-Commander Mark Beak, when he was presented with the Freedom of the Borough at the Palace Theatre.

It may seem strange that in 1919 Itchen should have its own separate peace celebrations, but that area did not officially become part of Southampton until the following year. The people to the east of the river have always valued their independence highly.

Laying the Foundation stone of the new Workhouse Infirmary, 1900

Foundry Lane School is born, 1901

An exciting Sunday on the Common, 1903

Honouring Lt.-Commander Mark Beak, V. C.

Itchen's Peace Day Celebrations — 30 July, 1919

The Pilgrim Fathers sailed from Southampton in 1620, and in 1920 the tercentenary was lavishly celebrated with a pageant and a water carnival, centred on the spot on the Western Esplanade from which the adventurers had set out. The citizens turned out in their thousands in support of notable guests. With Mayor Kimber we see in our picture the Earl of Birkenhead, the Marquis of Milford Haven, Major-General Seely and Col. Sir Harry Crichton.

Our last photograph leaps forward ten years — to Southampton's greatest foundation-stone laying ceremony. The date is 1st July. 1930, and the dream of Sidney Kimber (soon to become Sir Sidney) is becoming reality at last; H. R. H. the Duke of York is inaugurating the Civic Centre. Eighteen months later the Duke will return, this time accompanied by the Duchess, to perform the opening ceremony of the municipal block.

How could anyone present that day have guessed that before many years had passed this shy young man and his charming escort would (however reluctantly) become King and Queen? Or that their accession would lead to the lifting of the Monarchy to a pinnacle of national affection the like of which had been unknown for centuries?

CHANGE OF CLOTHES

We never lose our interest in changing fashions. I have just re-discovered, among the treasures of three Southampton families, some photographs which were taken during the early days of this century.

Comparing then with now, we notice that it is in men's clothing that the smallest changes have occurred. We are not surprised to find that women's dress has been revolutionised, but the greatest differences of all have been in children's garb.

Portrait paintings of Tudor, Stuart or Hanoverian times show that for centuries even small children were dressed as miniature versions of their elders. As late as the Victorian age the same ideas were followed. In today's customs there is a parallel. Particularly on informal occasions, the clothes worn by a boy or a girl will virtually be a replica of his or her parent's garments. Indeed, it is becoming increasingly common nowadays for a whole family to turn out in almost identical clothing. To the unisex trend we are now adding the unigeneration.

At the beginning of this century the usage of earlier times was overturned. Parents seemed determined to establish that a child was a child — not a little adult. It is true that young babies (both boys and girls) faced the world in very long dresses of the sort sometimes seen in modern days at church christenings. Later, however, they were 'tucked' (i.e. given shorter clothes). Even when he had learned to walk a small boy would still wear a frock. (The child in our picture of a family of three is a boy, not a girl. The present writer may as well confess: it is himself). The next stage came when, round about his third birthday, the little boy was 'breeched'.

Growing up, boys were dressed in clothing which bore little relation to that worn by adults — with one exception: the prestige of the Royal Navy was so great that sailor suits and hats were the most popular style for boys. This influence will be seen in several of our pictures.

There was another factor. Children had to be protected at all costs from the ravages of our climate. We notice that in two of our pictures the little boys wear thick, warm clothing, including woollen leggings. By later standards, they were being mollycoddled.

One boy's hoop and stick, incidentally, are a reminder of a whole world since lost — the world of all the fun at hand for boys and girls in carefree streets. Besides hoops, there were marbles and conkers and five-stones, peg-tops and tip cat, hopscotch and skipping, and all the lively group-games which demanded plenty of space. But that is another story.

The large sailor-type hats of the boys are reflected in the hat worn by the little girl with the doll. (How many girls — even tiny ones — play with dolls

FASHIONS — 1906

Young Family

Little boy, overdressed

Hoop boy

Four year old

MORE FASHIONS

Wedding Group, 1903

Little Miss Winsome, 1910

Growing up

today?). The clothing of the charming young lady with the muff bore little resemblance to that worn by her mother: it was unmistakably child clothing.

To return to that family of three: this tells us a great deal about women's dress of the period. Only the head, the hands and the wrists were uncovered. (And out of doors, even in the summer, hats and gloves would be worn).
"Oh, why do you walk through the fields in gloves,
Missing so much and so much?"

The figure was completely enveloped from the hidden shoes (or boots) to the top of the neck, where not infrequently whalebone caused much uncomfortable chafing of the flesh. (The V-neck was introduced in a blaze of excitement in 1913, when it was fiercely denounced as a health risk by doctors and as indecent by parsons. All this despite the fact that women's evening gowns were becoming more and more revealing). We notice here the elaborate flounces and the puffing of the tucked sleeves. Enormous quantities of material were needed for the more ambitious garments.

In our next picture the little boy seen earlier in white coat and hat is growing up fast. He now proudly shows off his new baby brother (born in 1910), who is enveloped in voluminous frock and petticoats. The boy's sailor-type collar is still in vogue, but we see one striking new feature: in stark contrast to the swaddling of the infant, his knees are bare. Was this following the example of the Boy Scouts, founded by Baden-Powell just three years before this photograph was taken? We are no longer spartan in the 1980s, when even in the summer months boys' legs are usually completely covered. Were our grandparents unduly severe on their children, or have we gone soft?

The boy wears lace-up boots. Shoes were not yet adopted for general use.

Finally, we go back in time to the wedding picture (1903), which really sums up the whole matter. The sombre clothes of the men are relieved here and there by a fancy waistcoat and a gold watch-chain. The bridesmaids' dresses follow the current exuberant style and their hats are of the extraordinary large flat kind then much favoured. A large hat is worn too by the little girl, who appears, by our standards, grossly overdressed. The boy's clothing is distinctly of a nautical cut.

Our grandparents and their children may have been smarter, but surely we are more comfortable.

AROUND THE BARGATE

There is nothing unusual about a town or a city shifting its centre of gravity as the years pass. Southampton's position, between the mouths of its two rivers, determined that such a move could be made only in a northerly direction.

In the Middle Ages, the town's accepted place of assembly was that part of the High Street (English Street) which fronted the Mayor's church, Holy Rood. Here the people came to listen to royal or municipal proclamations. Here was born — who knows just when? — the dancing on the asphalt with which successive generations welcomed in each New Year. This jolly custom survived up to the beginning of the present century.

By the time of Grandpa's boyhood, the natural meeting-place for celebrations had moved to the Bargate. Here, as far back as 1864, thousands had greeted the Italian national hero, Garibaldi. At this spot every year May Day was ushered in by a choir singing from the roof of the old gateway — an event happily revived in recent years by the excellent choir of King Edward VI School. That section of Above Bar to the north of the Bargate, in our own time has been widened and converted into a pedestrian precinct; but it was still narrow when it was packed with delirious citizens on the first Armistice Day, November 11th, 1918, and again shortly afterwards to acclaim the town's own V.C., Mark Beak.

We are here thinking about the immediate neighbourhood of the Bargate between the opening days of this century and the time, thirty years later, when work would begin on the construction of the circus to bring to an end a notorious bottleneck. In those years the demand that all traffic between Above Bar and Below Bar (an old name never heard today) must pass through one of three archways was a source of delight to the romantic and of exasperation to the enterprising.

It would have been impossible to find another spot in the town containing, within a few minutes' walk, a comparable hub of activity or, in business, as large a collection of household names.

Just south of the Bargate, at the entrance to East Street, stood All Saints Church, its classical Ionic facade hard up against the ever-thronged pavement; just north of the old gateway, set back from the street behind its handsome iron railings, was the Above Bar Congregational Church, for ever associated with the town's illustrious son, Isaac Watts. In the few hundred yards separating these two historic places of worship could be found, on the eastern side, the premises of Osborn, Larbalestier, Cleveland, Atkins, Burnett, Trippe, Gutteridge, Parkhouse, Laughland, Tanner, Gilbert. Opposite were the businesses of Misselbrook & Weston, Mayes, Johns, Stead & Simpson, Webb, Brown, Permain.

Landmarks just as familiar were the Gaiety Picture House, the Tivoli, the George Inn, the Cadena Café.

An amazing photograph of Southampton's 1906 May Day celebrations

The shopper taking a few steps further north or south would find the well-stocked windows of Rose & Co., Bastick, Wiseman, Fred Bailey, Emanuel, Shepherd & Hedger, Patstone, Cox & Son, Winter & Worth, Payne, Cox & Sharland, Pegler & Wyatt, Cheverton, Caplen and Horton, besides the Grosvenor Café and the headquarters of Andrews' noted carriage works.

The Star and the Dolphin Hotels are still with us, but the Crown in the High Street and the Royal in Above Bar have long since vanished.

Old pictures show us that, though externally the Bargate has suffered little change over the years, its interior and its immediate surroundings have been transformed. Now one of the city's attractive museums, sixty years ago the room above the archways was graced by the title of Guildhall and served as the magistrates' court. Firmly attached to the east was the quaint, old-world Pembroke Square. On the other side was the borough's police station in Bargate Street. This led westward, descending steeply to the Western Esplanade. This street's old dwelling-houses backed upon part of the northern medieval town walls (latterly revealed by road-widening here).

One of these houses was the home of the fire brigade chief, adjoining the fire station. (Transfer to St. Mary's Road took place in 1909). The brigade's horses were accommodated in the stables of the George Inn, opposite, so that often children who had joined their parents on shopping expeditions were thrilled at the sight and the sound of the fire-engines a-clang and the brass helmets a-gleam when there was a sudden emergency.

Our earlier lists of business pin-point a major difference between 'then' and 'now'. More often than not the people whose names appeared on the fascia-boards above the shop-windows could be found inside the premises, cheerfully supervising or even serving their customers.

Serving. Nowadays that kind of activity has almost disappeared. Furthermore, the name above the shop-fronts will now be found duplicated in the main streets of a dozen towns or cities throughout the kingdom. If we have gained in efficiency, our gain has been at the cost of personal contact's warm heart.

To every citizen, Southampton's most familiar scene.

The High Street's varied scene at the dawn of the century. Leisurely? Lazy? Sleepy even? Maybe, but warm and friendly.

And today, what of the warm heart of the city? In medieval times this was to be found at the High Street's Holy Rood. A hundred years ago — and less — the Bargate area was the undisputed hub of the town's corporate life.

Today? Is it some place further north? In June, 1945 the towns-people celebrated the end of hostilities in Europe by dancing joyfully in the forecourt of the Civic Centre. There, 31 years later, an ecstatic populace gathered to welcome home the cup-bearing Saints.

Even so, how many of us would be prepared to give an unhesitating reply to the question "Where today is the warm heart of Southampton?"

BY THE WATER'S EDGE

For once, we will approach a topic from an unusual angle — standing history on its head, as it were — proceeding from the 'now' to the 'then'.

In our first picture, taken recently, we have a scene familiar to most Southampton people. In the foreground is part of the Mayflower Park. In the middle distance are well-known landmarks — part of the Old Walls, the Tudor Merchants' Hall, the West Gate and the Royal Standard Inn. On the skyline, the spire of St. Michael's Church. Running from right to left between the new and the old is the Western Esplanade. This road is the crucial feature of our little study.

A familiar scene of to-day

Our second picture, an aerial view, takes in the same spot, but much, much more. Mayflower Park is easy to find (lower centre), with the Post House Hotel immediately to its right. Where is the Western Esplanade? As we know that it passes between the Corporation Central Baths and St. Michael's Church (bottom right-hand corner) we realise that here it is almost hidden by other buildings. It runs out of the picture on the right, to reappear further up alongside the railway line (Between it and the water, and sweeping in a great curve, is West Quay Road, in the Western Docks complex).

Continuing history in reverse, another aerial picture taken in the 1920s, reveals the magnitude of the task which faced the engineers who had to convert the vast acreage of water between the Royal Pier and Millbrook Point into the Western Docks. Here their great adventure has just begun. Once more our spot of special interest is in the bottom right-hand corner.

47

The water-line is pushed back (Below): the great docks' extension begins in the 1920's

Western Shore when townspeople could walk by the water's edge

Before we pass on, we notice the huge peninsula in the distance — a reminder of the extent of a further and more recent great enterprise, the container docks extension. But that is another story.

Our fourth picture is a simpler affair altogether, but then those were simpler times, for we are taking a big backward jump to the early 1900s. On our right is our old friend the Western Esplanade, appropriately named in those days, for on summer evenings thousands of townspeople loved to stroll there by the tree-lined water's edge.

The promontory in the centre, reaching out opposite the West Gate (here partially hidden by the curve of the shoreline) was part of the old West Quay. This quay, which appears on the Ordnance Survey map of 1846, was once dominated by boat-yards, and from here passengers embarked on the ferry to Cracknore Hard.

But what is the link between our final picture and the four which have gone before? We notice here that waves lap the stone sea-wall. Allowing for the curve of the river, one of the buildings on the left could well be the West Gate. To the immediate left of the handsome house is a stretch of old stone wall, behind which we see one end of a shabby building. Is this the Tudor Merchants' Hall?

The truth is that we are looking at a house which once stood almost at the centre of our first picture. This building had been variously known as Westgate House, Marett's, the French House and finally Madame Maes' House. The site, certainly occupied as far back as 1730, was first the home

49

and shipyard of one George Rowcliffe (suitable name?). A later owner, Charles Marett, built the stone sea-wall and turned the shipyard into a garden, which went down to the water's edge.

Eventually the property was inherited by Hannah Winifred Maes, widow of Joseph Emile Maes of Nantes. Her children sold it to the Southampton Corporation in the 1890s. Finally the house was demolished and a road was constructed from the pier entrance to the old West Quay and beyond. This was the birth of the Western Esplanade.

Madame Maes was loved by all who knew her for her unfailing kindness. She gave lavishly to the poor people living in Simnel Street and the surrounding courtyards, often parting with the clothes that she was actually wearing at the time of her visits to their mean homes.

Among the many children to visit her and to play in her garden were the future Admiral Earl Jellicoe and his brother, who then lived in East Park Terrace.

The construction of the house was unique. Our picture suggests that its three storeys were built hard up against the ancient wall, but that is only part of the truth. The house's rear section of one storey (level with the middle storey of the front) was also attached to the old wall — on the other side!) That part of the house faced Cuckoo Lane (still with us), separated from it by a large back garden.

The house enveloped the first and second of the archways of the stone wall, seen just right of centre in our first picture. Indeed, the first archways formed an alcove in one of the rooms. Presumably doorways were cut in the thick walls to give access between the two parts of the building. We need not feel in the least dubious about this evidence, for the 1846 Ordnance Survey map shows clearly the two halves of the house, one half on each side of the wall, and the spacious gardens similarly separated.

Fifty years ago E. Mitchell ("Townsman" of the Southern Daily Echo), researching the story of this old house, quoted many details supplied by a Mr. W. F. Gubbins, of Millbrook Road, whose memories went back a further fifty years. We like to think that these two worthy gentlemen would not resent our setting down once again the result of their labours. Would they not be pleased to know that the people of Southampton share their interests, all these years later?

Today, in front of the old walls, a horse-trough, dated 1900, is inscribed "To the loving memory of Madame Maes and other members of her family whose house stood on this site and was built and occupied by them A.D. 1700-1900".

Its usefulness came to an end long ago, but it is an affectionate reminder of a gracious lady and her handsome house.

Madame Maes' home at Western Esplanade long ago

OLD NORTHAM

During recent decades few places have been left untouched by change.

Parts of many larger towns have been changed beyond recognition by a combination of factors: the drift of families away from town centres; the encroachment of industry; the domination of gargantuan multi-stores; war damage — and above all the insatiable demands of the motor-car.

No town or city has suffered more severely than Southampton, where the processes of change still march on unabated.

It would be difficult to find any other district in the city which has undergone so complete an alteration as Northam. Indeed, one may justly refer to the Old Northam, of which so little now remains, and the New Northam which has taken its place.

Old Northam existed for just 100 years. While it is true that there had been boat-building on the river-bank as far back as the closing years of the 17th century, followed by the setting up of allied activities — timber yards, coal wharves, a smithy — and the construction of quays, true settlement did not begin until the building of humble dwellings in Millbank Street in the 1840s. This was followed at varying pace by development westward. Accommodation was thus provided for men employed (all too often casually) at the newly-opened town docks, besides those working nearer home.

The other revolutionary event of the time, the coming of the railway, contributed to the shaping of the newly-burgeoning district by fixing its western boundary (any Northamite will react fiercely to the occasional attempts to consider anything beyond the railway line as part of Northam, pointing out that such districts belong to either Nicholstown or Newtown. It is true that the Old Farmhouse Inn at Mount Pleasant had once been a Northam landmark, but the coming of the railway and the passage of the years changed all that).

Down river from Old Northam lay the populous district of Chapel, the two being separated by the tiny buffer state with the now-vanished name of Crabniton. Thus, virtually enclosed on all sides, Northam evolved a character all its own. The place has more than once been likened to a village, and the comparison is not far-fetched.

In 1873 the local people welcomed a sign of the growing importance of their suburb: the opening of their own railway station, Northam Junction.

We tend to forget the part played by the railway in the daily life of the people 100 years ago. One simple illustration: my grandparents lived throughout the latter half of the last century in St. Denys. For an excursion to town they had three alternative routes. First, on foot, crossing the railway line into Dukes Road (that was before the construction of the footbridge and the horseshoe roadway) and walking through Bevois Valley; second, from Portswood by horse-bus — later horse-tram; and third (the favourite) by train from St. Denys — first named Portwood — Station to Northam or Southampton West.

Years passed — the railway declined — in the 1950s Northam Station disappeared.

From 1910 Northam was linked by tram with the centre of the town at the old Clock Tower site. Until 1929 the traveller, arriving at the Northam terminus and wishing to proceed further, paid his copper at the toll-gate and walked across the narrow iron Northam Bridge, which had been built in 1889 in replacement of the original wooden structure of 1797. The present busy concrete bridge was opened in 1954.

Reference has been made to Northam's village-like character. As in most villages, corner shops satisfied most of its basic needs (often in penny numbers). Its many pubs catered for its deep-throated communal thirst. Its parish church and its little chapels and mission halls did their best to respond to its spiritual yearnings. Its schools, with staffs activated by a down-to-earth, no-nonsense brand of sympathy, maintained a firm discipline within and a healthy respect beyond their walls.

The story of the schools reflects the growth of the district. In Britain, the 19th century was a period of rapid growth in population. By 1870, nationally, the average number of children per family was six. Even allowing for the high death-rate (sadly, here even higher than the town's average) Northam did not lag behind this general trend. The original National Schools, opened in mid-century on ground between York Street and Clarence Street, were replaced in the 1890s by the much larger Board School buildings in Kent Street, parts of which remain today. These provided accommodation for 560 boys, 600 girls and 540 infants.

Thus Northam had the largest school in the town, catering for one of the smallest areas of intake.

From earliest days Northam people developed a way of life which was at once independent and yet interdependent. If neighbours were not always loved, at least they were understood, and should strangers dare to intrude, ranks were closed as if by magic. Reaction to sickness, injury, bereavement, disaster (and no place suffered more deeply from the Titanic tragedy than Northam) might well be clumsy — even crude — but at least it was warm and sincere. There was no room for the supersensitive, for everybody understood that, whatever tongues might utter, the hearts of Joe Blunt and his missus were in the right place.

And there were all too many occasions which called for sympathy. Life for

The old tram terminus with Northam Bridge beyond

the majority was tough. During periods of recession (and such could be far more devastating than the set-backs of our modern times) Northam bore more than its share of the brunt. Until well into the 20th century many streets, houses, tiny back yards were annually at the mercy of severe flooding. For much of those hundred years the place was shamefully neglected in respect of sanitation. In consequence Northam ranked high in the tables of illness, disease, mortality.

Yet, despite the many disadvantages and discouragements, it would be difficult to find elsewhere a sense of loyalty to match the attachment of former Northam people to the scenes of their childhood. Today middle-aged men and women will recall with the pride their links with the tiny terraced cottages and the drab, humble streets of that close-knit, self-contained community.

Nothing could better illustrate the spirit of the place than our photograph of poor but happy children massed together in a Northam street in the mid-1920s. There is no stand-offishness here. Babes and big brothers and sisters, neighbours and buddies, the shabby and the spick and span, all pack together in cheerful obedience to the call of the itinerant street photographer.

The first cracks appeared in the fabric of normal life in the early autumn of 1940 when, after the deceptive months of the phony war, followed by the epic days of the Battle of Britain, Northam felt at first hand the grim reality

York Street children, about 1925

of aerial warfare. The climax came during the nights of late November and early December. Then, in common with the people of Southampton's ancient heartland — High Street and Above Bar and their immediate surroundings — most of the brave, stubborn people of Northam were forced at last to leave the tragic remnants of their ruined homes — many of them for ever.

A true story from those grim times is worth repeating:

"A grey dawn breaks after a night of horror. Emerging from the shelter, a middle-aged Northam housewife finds her humble home virtually destroyed. Though when viewed from the street it appears almost intact, inside the scene is one of pitiable carnage.

Her friends try to persuade her that she must, for the present at least, seek refuge elsewhere. In vain. When authority puts its foot down, she grudgingly gives in.

But not without delay. She pushes open the creaky, tottering front door. Fighting her way through the chaos which yesterday was her home, she manages to reach the tiny kitchen. She returns with a pail of water, a scrubbing brush, hearthstone and a rag. While her friends stand impatiently by, she drops to her knees and carefully, lovingly, cleans and whitens the front doorstep.

Then, and then only, she agrees to leave"

That is a typical example of the spirit of Old Northam.

The sensation of a Northam child, now grown up and returning from afar after many years, hopeful of rediscovering old haunts, would be one of utter bewilderment. Apart from an ancient row of cottages here and there, a lonely pub bravely facing a new world, the gasworks, the road over the railway line, he would find little to bring reality to those dreams often dreamed in distant places.

We have used the numbers of children attending the schools in the past as evidence of the population density of Old Northam. Nothing could more dramatically illustrate the recent changes in the district than the comparable figures for today.

During 1984 the few children of middle-school-age — numbering about 60 — left the classroom so well remembered by parents, grand-parents and great-grand-parents — to boost similarly fallen numbers at St. Mary's School (formerly known as Ascupart). Northam school itself catered for only 50 boys and girls under the age of 8. The few children above the age of 12, of course, attended the appropriate comprehensive school.

New Northam — trim, smart, sophisticated — is building up its own character (its latest development is the exciting Shamrock Quay).

MARKET DAY
A Backward Glance

Old George was an early riser. He had to be, for in farming the sluggard has always gone to the wall, even in those leisurely days before World War I. Occasionally on a Wednesday morning, however, rising had to be earlier than ever. His jolly wife, Harriet, never complained, for to her there was nothing more enjoyable than a trip to market.

Not that she saw much of the market. That was George's province, but the bustle of Southampton's main streets and the ever-changing liveliness of the shops were her idea of heaven, supplying, during the weeks which followed, ample material for happy, animated recall.

At the crack of dawn old Matthew had been seen safely on his way with the dozen or so sheep selected for sale. With him went the lad Joe. Joe was a great help, but of even greater value — in fact quite indispensible — was the faithful, sagacious collie Scotty.

On their way, as the eastern sky rapidly lightened, they trudged down lanes which ran between high dog-rose and honeysuckle-bespangled hedges, along dusty main roads, across narrow stone bridges, through villages just rousing from the night's slumber — now holding up muttering drivers of vans and farm-carts; now forcing cyclists to dismount; now, through the stupid aberrations of the flock, taxing the instinctive skills of Scotty, raising the ire of old Matthew and provoking the shrill, angry cries of young Joe.

Back at home, before relishing their hearty breakfast, George and Harriet had daily chores to attend to. Young George and his strapping sister, Rose, could be relied upon to look after the routine of the farm, but Dad liked to do the milking, while Mum never left to anyone else the care of her chickens.

At last all was ready. Harriet stood back and nodded her affectionate approval to George, who was at his smartest in sturdy greenish tweed jacket, neat breeches, shiny stout brown boots, highly polished gaiters and meticulously-brushed billycock hat; in his tie his favourite gold fox's head tiepin.

Jack, the younger son, stood by the chestnut mare Flo, as the couple climbed into their seats in the gig. There was a quiet word to Flo, a wave to the family and they were off.

Almost an hour later, having passed through the straggling rural districts of Eling and Totton, they crossed the Test by way of the ancient narrow stone bridges. As they moved through Redbridge and into Millbrook they heard the ringing of bells and they overtook children on their way to school.

They passed the cottage, set with its neighbours well back from the road and bearing the strange sign, famous for miles around: OSS OIL. Made redundant by its immaculate successor, old St. Nicholas Church still stood, ivy-clad and rather forlorn, behind its lych-gate.

To their right ran the railway line. Beyond, the widening waters of the Test merged into the even wider Southampton Water; ahead soared the tall coloured funnels of ships resting between their long voyages to and from the Americas, the Cape, the Far East, the Antipodes.

As they passed the Southampton West Station with its tall clock tower, the London train, billowing forth its cloud of white cotton wool, chug-chugged out and plunged into the blackness of the tunnel.

On into the Western Esplanade they rode. On their left, the trim Victorian Weymouth Terrace. Opposite, the water lapped unceasingly below the edge of the shore-line pavement.

They reached the town's ancient stone walls, passed the Royal Standard Inn, passed the West Gate, through which Henry V is said to have led his troops on their way to Agincourt, though this would mean little to George and' his Harriet.

By now the chestnut mare was thirsty, so there was a pull-up at the roadside trough. This had been erected to honour the memory of Madame Maes and her family, whose handsome house had once stood just here. To make matters easier for Flo, George manouevred mare and gig so that both stood at right angles to the trough. Among other road-users nobody worried about the obstruction: those were tolerant days.

Several lively boys, climbing on an old cannon which stood near the Stella Memorial, suddenly realised that the ringing of the bells had ceased. Scared, they tumbled down and raced helter-skelter towards French Street, fearful of the master's wrath.

Our travellers drew level with the Town Quay. Approaching them, a train steamed along the sub-line from the Terminus Station, conveying Isle of Wight-bound passengers to the little railway station on the Royal Pier, and the paddle steamer.

George directed Flo into the busy High Street, home of many inns and premises with powerful maritime connections — ship's chandlers, rope and sail makers, naval outfitters, shipping agents, fruit merchants. Straw-hatted students, preparing for morning lectures, were entering the imposing portals of the Hartley University College. Opposite, local government clerks were beginning the day's work at the Audit House.

At the top of Bridge Street (later to be renamed Bernard Street) they pulled up, and George gallantly helped his wife down. She would spend several

"On into the Western Esplanade"

"Southampton West Station with its tall clock tower"

Climbing on an old cannon

"The little railway station on the Royal Pier"

happy hours exploring the shops, while he enjoyed the rest of the morning at the cattle market, near the Central Bridge and the Terminus Station, interrupted by the occasional withdrawal with his cronies to their favourite hostelry in Terminus Terrace.

Harriet took her time, savouring every minute. She paused to drop a few coins into the tin of the patient blind man who, as ever, sat with his dog in front of the railings outside Holy Rood. As she did so, the quaint little jacks on the tower struck the quarter.

She gazed admiringly at the handsome Dolphin Hotel with its generous pot-bellied bow windows and at its sister the Star, beyond St. Lawrence Church. The shops were larger now, leading up to Shepherd and Hedger's where she appraised, not without some envy, the latest styles in furnishings.

Beyond the massive columns of All Saints she crossed the road, threading her way carefully through the ambling horse traffic. A top-hatted commissionaire, having delicately assisted an elegant dowager to alight from her carriage, was now ushering her through the entrance of Messrs. Mayes' shop.

On a past visit there Harriet had felt more than impressed — even daunted — by the attentions of the well-meaning but ponderous shop-walkers. "More at home in a cathedral", she told her old friend Lizzie afterwards.

So, on to Richard Allen's, for she had a sweet tooth and nobody could equal their confectionery. Another attraction from just hereabouts — the heavenly scents which always announced Luce's perfume shop.

61

"The busy High Street"

She walked through the western pedestrian passageway of the Bargate just as, almost within touching distance, a clanging open-topped tramcar entered the central archway.

She drifted along Above Bar, earlier memories coming to life again. Webb's for trunks. Brown the butcher; scuffing about its sawdust-carpeted floor was a genial figure in striped apron and straw hat, the soul of rosy rotundity. Boots Cash Chemists, bright with huge bottles of coloured water. The diary, in whose window was a china swan, its hollow body filled with fresh duck-eggs. On the corner of Portland Street, Messrs. Toogood proudly proclaimed themselves as "The King's Seedsmen".

Among the shops, other buildings. The Palace Theatre, with glossy photographs of visiting artistes. In contrast, the staid Church of Christ. The Alexandra Picture house advertised the latest Tom Mix film. The influential Royal Southampton Yacht Club. In the lofty red-brick Prudential Buildings a bevy of foreign consulates, presided over by swarthy senors with exotic names, from Argentina, Brazil, Mexico, Panama, Peru.

The Clock Tower reminded Harriet that time was speeding by. Plummer Roddis, Dunsfords, Tyrrell & Green must await a later visit. As she crossed the road she glanced over her shoulder at the old ladies sitting placidly in the beautiful garden of Thorner's Charity alms-houses. At the Clock Tower trough a hefty horse, attached to a water-spraying, dust-laying cart, was slaking its thirst.

She turned south, then passed old Palmerston in his park, passed Smith Bradbeer's, W. H. Smith's, the Halford Cycle Company, the Sussex Hotel. Fascinated, she paused to watch the fantastic toffee-making machine of Butter Creams.

She could never resist the appeal of mute pathos. Every time she saw, standing in the gutter, a gaunt bedraggled figure bearing a tray she had to stop, even though she knew that at home she had boxes of matches and bootlaces by the dozen.

She crossed narrow Pound Tree Lane, passed the Royal Hotel, its elegant iron balcony resplendent with geraniums and petunias. Then in succession Andrews Brothers' carriage works, keeping alive the famous name of the founder, old Richard; Wiseman's the art shop; Rose's for fancy goods; the Above Bar Congregational Church. A bespectacled old man in shabby claw-hammer coat and faded bowler hat was bemusedly examining the bargains outside H. M. Gilbert's bookshop. Hanover Buildings. Parkhouse the jeweller. Gutteridge's for toys. Old Pembroke Square, and so back through the Bargate.

Ahead lay East Street, Harriet's favourite haunt. Ten minutes were spent in the penny bazaar, happily gathering attractive trifles for the grandchildren, besides several surprising items for the farm kitchen.

Past York Buildings, where some young townee relatives would be at school. She remembered little Tommy saying that, as there was no playground, the children spent their "playtimes" in the nearby parks. It seemed that important people from London disapproved of this, though to Harriet it seemed a sensible arrangement.

The atmosphere was filled with pungent odours from Cooper's brewery.

Any hankering which she might have had about a visit to the Southampton Picture House, the tiny pioneer cinema, would have been in vain, for the doors would not open until evening-time.

As Harriet passed the flagstoned forecourt of the Wesleyan Methodist Church, at the moment deserted, she recalled a night scene there, when she had been spending a few days with cousin Louisa, who lived nearby. Then, beneath a guttering flare stood a stall, where bowler-hatted Mr. Goodman dispensed cheap china and glassware and all manner of cheap household goods — and not least the penny 'lucky bags', filled with attractive novelties for the children. This morning he was doubtless touring the suburbs with his little donkey cart.

The high spot of the day came at last: Edwin Jones' store. In terms of cash spent, Harriet's visit was not especially noteworthy, but in pleasure gained the experience was beyond measure. Our visitor wandered from one department to another without thought of fatigue (that would come later), entranced by the variety of the attractive display of goods for sale.

Breathing a quiet sigh of regret that time was speeding away altogether too fast, she forced herself to move on.

Just one more adventure before, as arranged, she joined up with George — a roam down that exciting backwater, Canal Walk ("The Ditches"). What a mingling of people was here! The sharp-eyed traders; the poorly-clad folk from the tangled maze of dingy courts and alleys which made up the background to this crowded neighbourhood; the bewildered lascars from the ships in the docks nearby; the well-to-do shoppers whose interest was merely one of curiosity; the dooching bare-foot urchins, slippery as quicksilver, always on the alert, for the school attendance officers ("The school board men") might be on the prowl.

One more stop, for a pound of sausages (George's favourite breakfast) and she hurried on.

George was waiting for her at their rendezvous — the Old Red Lion Inn in the High Street. So, if tradition is to be believed, twice in one day our couple had made remote contact with Henry V, for we are told that it was in the Red Lion that the conspirators against the life of their king faced their trial.

All this was many worlds away from the thoughts of our simple, down-to-earth old friends as they tucked into their roast beef, horseradish sauce and Yorkshire pudding and quaffed their golden ale.

At last, the mare refreshed by good stabling, they set out on the return journey (Old Matthew, the lad and the collie had accepted the offer of a lift in a kindly neighbour's cart, the dog sleeping like a log every inch of the way).

As our couple jog-trotted back beneath the westering sun, between those familiar dog-rose and honeysuckle-bespangled hedges, old Harriet's double chin rested comfortable on her ample bosom. Her breathing had become a steady, gentle snore. Beside his partner sat George, well content. In his capacious pockets jingled a goodly number of golden sovereigns but, beyond that, he had been enriched by a day's lively companionship with his cronies. He was awake, but only just. No matter, the chestnut mare knew her way home.

Somnolence must be contagious. I awoke with a start as my book — a 70-year-old illustrated guide to Southampton — slid from my knees and crashed to the floor. As I retrieved it hurriedly, relieved to find it undamaged, I reflected that distance — in time as in space — always lends enchantment to the view.

"The old Red Lion"

PICTURES
FROM
THE PAST

As the years pass, a few places remain unchanged, but more often recognition is difficult — even impossible.

In the "Then and Now" pairs that follow on the next few pages, the recent photographs are by Jim Shepperd.

To start, can you place this 1890 (c) photograph?
(The answer is on page 71).

The lower High Street in the 1880's — and the same area a hundred years later.

East Park Terrace in the 1930's. It was entirely residential. (Below); East Park Terrace in the 1980's — now the site of the Central Health Clinic and Institute of Higher Education.

Upper Above Bar Street, looking towards the Junction. (Prospect Place): Thorner's Charities on the extreme left. Upper Moira Place extreme right with Redcliffe House (home of Robert Chipperfield) immediately south of Tyrrell and Green's shop. Early 20th century.

Below: Above Bar Street in the 1980s — one evening!

The Junction — summer mid-day, early 20th century.

The Junction — a summer evening in the mid — 1980's

The Answer:

The Picture on p.69 —Did you know where it was?

The answer — *Above Bar, looking south towards the Bargate. And here is the same scene in the 1980s*

Below: A pleasant photograph of Barge Banks, immediately upstream from Woodmill, early 20th century

50 Years Ago

*Opposite: Waiting for fares,
the cabbies doze in Canute Road.*

*Below: Chapel members have a day
out.*

The working horse slakes his thirst in Shirley High Street.

Southampton once had its own beach — a very stony one — on the Western Shore, near Millbrook Station.

The Ordnance Survey Offices at the lower end of The Avenue, was one of Southampton's best known buildings. Many people paused to check their watches by its clock, even though it did not always tell the correct time!

Southampton's first purpose-built public library — art gallery at the junction of London Road and Cumberland Place. It was opened in 1892.

SPRING PRANK!

The Avenue

One morning in 1908 the people of Hampshire awoke to see snow falling heavily. The date was the 25th April (repeat, April). The fall continued throughout the morning, the flakes soon becoming the largest most people had ever seen. By midday, in much of the county, the ground was covered to a depth of two feet, and still the storm raged on, unabated.

As this was a Saturday, most of the schools were closed, but in those days Saturday morning was a regular working period, and so much activity was brought to a standstill. Southampton's dockland was virtually paralysed. Tradesmen wearily led their unharnessed horses back to their stables, leaving vans and carts stranded. Trees collapsed beneath the weight of the snow. The few tram-cars which had set out were abandoned in their tracks.

All very exciting, but when night-time came, cruel fate took a hand. In the Solent, in the teeth of the continuing blizzard, two vessels — the U. S. Liner "St. Paul" and H.M.S. "Gladiator", en route for Portsmouth, collided, resulting in 27 men perishing in the icy waters.

If all this seems like a fantastic dream, a nightmare even, we can thank the enterprising unknown photographer who preserved the reality in a series of beautiful pictures.

Western Shore — looking south from Forest View.

The Esplanade and the Royal Pier

Not a soul in sight.

76

Mr Kimber, landlord of Pembroke Hotel, Pembroke Square, beside the Bargate, takes stock

The Bargate begins to recover.

A tram car abandoned at the Junction

The Clock Tower — lonely sentinel

BEST YEARS?

School days were not always spent behind desks

The year: 1902. The place: The Dell football ground. The occasion: celebration of the Coronation of King Edward VII. As St. Mark's School is seen above the East Stand, perhaps the children watching the ascent of a grotesque gas balloon were pupils of that school? Who knows?

Freemantle's headmaster, staff and 130 boys on a ramble through the New Forest on 20 October, 1907.

(Below): Foundry Lane boys assemble to salute the flag on Empire Day — watched by parents. The year? Believed to be 1911.

June, 1914 — *Boys of Taunton's School entertained by Mr. W. F. G. Spranger in the grounds of Uplands, recently purchased as their new school site. Within two months, the country was at war with the Germans and the move from New Road was delayed by ten years.*

Boys and girls of Swaythling Senior School (later Hampton Park) co-operate in a play based on life in medieval Southampton. Producer: Mr. P. J. Crickmore; scenery by Mr. S. de Grouchy. The year: 1938.

1936 — Miss A. M. Platt welcomes pupils of the Girls' Grammar School to their new building in Hill Lane on the school's transfer from Argyle Road.

1947 — Taunton's School, back at Highfield after World War II evacuation, presents "The "Arcadians," the first of a number of memorable post-war productions. Producer: Dr. H. M. King (later Lord Maybray-King).

1952: Swaythling Senior Girls School — a visit to Tuileries Gardens, Paris.

1957 — Beechwood Junior School presents a musical based on "The Pied Piper of Hamelin." Here is a part of the huge cast.

The 4th year forms and staff of Swaythling Girls' School on a visit to the House of Commons where they were received by Dr. Horace King, M.P — c. 1957.

1911: Freemantle School Cup-winning football team, with the headmaster Mr. A. J. H. Marshall, Mr. W. Stickland, and Rev. E. Jellicoe (Rector and brother of the famous Admiral).

Southampton Schools Football team, 1932.

1948: Northam Junior School — winners of the Junior School's Cricket Cup.

SCHOOL FOOTBALL

The year 1932 was a peak for Southampton Schools' football. The boys played Manchester in the national competition's final, drawing first-away and then again at the Dell. The Cup was held alternatively six months with each team.

Opposite we see the team, reserves and teachers. Teachers: (L to R) Standing: Messrs. Gosham, Coar, Charlton, Gane, Carless, Mew, Duncan, Walters. Seated: Messrs. Watson, Prevett, Wood, Newton.
Boys: King, Johnson, Crook, Stansbridge, Page, Lanham, Harris, Church, Buxton, Catlin, Jewett, Brown, Griggs and Petts.

1954 — King Edward VI School hockey team. Standing: (L to R) Leonard Mann, master-in-charge 1st XI, Graham Rogers, Brian Mackay, Tony Roberts, Mike Ventham, Les Dear, Robin Lawson, master-in-charge hockey. Sitting (L to R) Malcolm Fiddes, Ray Wetton, Geoff Wilkinson (capt.), Mike Wheeler, Ray Paull. In front: Terry Carter, Don Milsom.

VANISHED SIGHTS

In the opening days of the century, Mr. Harold Goldsmith, of Bitterne Park, was a motoring pioneer.

Opposite: His historic Sunbeam Mabley.

Below: His second venture — the Turner-Miesse steam-driven car. Catching fire on Beaulieu Heath it was towed home by horse and cart.

This was revolutionary in the 1920's. The PT class had removed not only their caps but even their jackets. (Swaythling Mixed School).

The old organ-grinder has Bitterne High Street to himself.

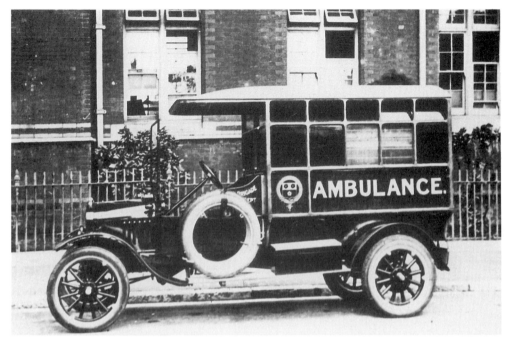

One of the Southampton Fire Brigade's first motor ambulances.

GPO parcel delivery before motor vans took over.

Above: Before the invention of mechanical monsters, roads were made with shiny spades and much sweat.

Opposite: The telegraph boy. He rode a red-framed bicycle and carried his telegrams in buff envelopes in the wallet of his belt.

At No. 368 Portswood Road, Southampton, Mr. Stanfield sold basic house-hold goods and delivered coal, coke, briquettes, firewood, oil and corn by donkey cart.

This contraption swept the loose dust to the side of the road to be collected by men with huge shovels. (Below): In dry summer spells the sprinkler was brought out, leaving behind the unique smell of damp dust.

Southampton's first motorised fire engine, 1908. It created great excitement when it first went into action.

The darker side — at the rear of dwellings in Lime Street, Threefield Lane area, early 1930's.

THE HEART STILL BEATS

63 SOUTHAMPTON. — *Above Bar.* — LL.

Above Bar in the era of the horse and tram.

Above Bar — peaceful prosperity in the 1930's

The 1940's — the aftermath of the savagery of the German raids.

The 1950's — patient recovery.

DOCKLAND

This book would be incomplete — one is tempted to say meaningless without mention of that feature of Southampton's life which, continuing unbroken during many centuries, has made the city's name known throughout the world — its role as a port.

The Empress Dock, so named in 1890 to honour its opener — Queen Victoria.

Opposite: The pedestrians came into their own in the 1980's.

A heart-breaking event which Southampton will never forget — the Titanic sets out on her first and last voyage, April 1912.

Troops await departure for a distant Empire outpost. At the back, an early Union Castle liner. Early 1900's.

Indispensables — a group of crane drivers, early 1920's.

This photograph was taken from a Super-marine flying boat. The nearest jetty was specially built during World War I to link troop-ships with the railway system.

Two fine sights which will never be seen again — the "Queen Elizabeth" and the Ocean Terminal.

Southampton port has always played a major part in war-time emergencies. Here the barrage balloons protect vessels from sudden attack in World War II.

Prelude to D. Day. One small section of the huge concentration of tank landing craft, awaiting the fateful invasion of Normandy — June, 1944.

HALLS

Over the next few pages there are glimpses of some of the buildings which, in their time, were well-known to the people of Southampton and the surrounding area.

The Hartley Institution in Lower High Street was the venue for concerts, public meetings, debates and exhibitions. It was also the forerunner of the University of Southampton.

The Bungalow Café, just below the Junction, was a favourite rendezvous for many years. Away back in 1905 it advertised: "For the convenience of ladies, shopping, bicycles and parcels may be left."

Here is part of Albion Congregational Church's oriental bazaar, held in the Royal Victoria Rooms in Portland Terrace. With the neighbouring Coliseum, the Rooms were in great demand for varied functions.

The Hippodrome, in Ogle Road, celebrated the end of World War 1 by inviting all Southampton men who had served with the Forces, with their families, to special free performances.

A young audience packed the Alexandra Cinema 60 years ago.

ON THE OUTSKIRTS

(Above): Hamble 80 years ago and (below) Upper Midanburg Lane coming down to the junction with Cobden Avenue.

Two village scenes at the beginning of this century. Where are they? (Top) West End; (Below) Rownhams.

(Above): Glenfield farmhouse stood about where Glenfield Avenue now meets Mousehole Lane. For many years the land beyond the River Itchen and towards Bitterne and West End was was devoted to farming. (Below): This stretch of Woodville Lane, running from the end of Manor Farm Road, Bitterne Park to Woodville has since been transformed by the making of Riverside Park on the left and the pitch and putt course on the right.

ANCIENT PEACE

On rare occasions we are fortunate enough to find resistance to the headlong rush of a changing world.

North Stoneham Church, notable for its one-hand clock, recently celebrated 900 years of worship on this site.

(Below): Surely the founders of ancient South Stoneham Church were divinely inspired when they chose this quiet, peaceful spot for their devotions.

THIS STONE WAS LAID BY
Mᴿ E. W. GADD.
JUNE 30 ᵀᴴ 1890

Postscript

On earlier pages, mention has been made of the laying of foundation stones.

Sadly, despite the evidence of this photograph and the fact that the author can look back upon many summers, he has been unable to convince his friends about his stone-laying adventure in 1890.

Well, the truth will out. Grandfather Gadd was Esau William, a dedicated if somewhat prickly member of the Bitterne Wesleyan Methodist Chapel — choirmaster, no less, complete with tuning fork. When a new hall was to be added to the old building in Chapel Street (now Dean Road) he was invited to officiate. The chapel vanished long ago, but the extension, still displaying the historic stone, remains as the St. John Ambulance headquarters.

Reflected glory, indeed!